TIPS TO BECOME A SUCCESSFUL LAWYER

A TORCH BEARER TO

LEGAL PROFESSIONALS

PRASOON KUMAR MISHRA

I DEDICATE THIS BOOK TO…..

My Parents who are my real God, My Brothers,
Sisters & Relatives who are my Emotional Strength
My Wife who is my Soul mate And my dear Son.

Contents

1.

Personal Track Of A Lawyer

Good Listener

Good Speaker

Ways Of Representation

Monetary Alertness

Don't Run For Or Run After The Clients

Watch The Court Proceedings

Avoid Close Intimacy

2.

Essential Legal Skills

Understand Case And Its Jurisdiction

Drafting

Get Certified Copy Of Your Case File

Professional Attitude

AOR (Advocate On Record)

Patent Agent

Try To File PIL Cases

Supreme Court Of India Guideline For PIL

3.

Develop And Maintain Contacts

Five Persons Per Day Rule

ARC Triangle

Attending Functions And Seminars

Try To Organize Seminars

Handling Cases Of Your Relations And
Close Friends

Politics And A Lawyer

Art Of Influencing People

4.

Continuous Legal Education

Legal Education

Habits Of Studying Leading Cases

Preface

The journey of writing this book starts with the concept of success mantra in the profession of advocacy and lack of any proper guidance or book in this regard. A law graduate of even one of the top schools and passing with flying colour seems to be failure in real advocacy work. Because no any law school teach those techniques. These techniques acquired with the experience and by giving long time to the profession with dedication. This book is divided into many parts with subheadings and descriptions which clears the mind of a budding lawyer about what to do and how to do, to become successful in the profession. Because it a unique profession where professional ethics counts much to be followed, as dignity of a lawyer is very much important. The representation in the form of this book is nothing but a collection of experiences got by the author and his understanding the for the tips i.e. "Tips to Become a Successful Lawyer" The author will feel obliged for tendering constructive suggestions from any quarters for the improvement of the book in onward editions. The author hopes that the book will serve the need of readers to be successful in his onward journey of legal profession of advocacy. With good wish to all my readers for their progressive professional step ahead.

Delhi 06-06-2020   Prasoon Kumar Mishra

CHAPTER ONE

Personal Track of a Lawyer

1.Personal Track of a Lawyer

" Always be yourself, express yourself, have faith in yourself, do not go out side and look for successful personality and duplicate it" – Bruce Lee

Good Listener

To become a successful lawyer, this point is most important point, because it only your listening habit, which provides you a better understanding your client and his/her case. Until and unless you listen the entire case very carefully, you may not be able to produce your case before the honourable court in better manner. The listening habit is not only beneficial to produce your case before the court in a effective manner but you get other benefits also through your this skill. It increases greater number of friends and social networks, improved self-esteem and confidence, higher grade at academic work and even better health and general well-being. Increasing friends and social network ultimately helps you in your profession of advocacy as more you are acquainting with the people, more case you get. The studies have also shown that this habit is also very good for your heath point of view, as whereas the speaking raises blood pressure, listening brings it down. In this way it is also a method for a lawyer to have pressure at normal index, as the lawyer has to speak before the court which brings increased pressure. Here I am emphasising you that you have to listen the case, not just to hear the case for the development of your legal profession's skill, as the listening is not the same as hearing. Hearing refers to the sound that you hear, whereas listening requires more then that. It requires focus. Listening means paying attention not only to the case of your client, but how it is told, use of language and voice, and how the person uses his or her body. Because marking on these very things, you can better understand your client regarding truth ness of the case and thus better understanding the case of your client. Thus being a good listener you develop your understanding in a better way to understand the verbal and non-verbal massages of your client. For your professional development you must have not listen your clients only but try to listen the argument of the leading lawyer of your locality, before the court of law and make it a regular habit. Because it not only helps you to increase your knowledge of law but also guide you how to argue your case in a better manner before the court. It also helps you to learn a good physical gesture which you can adopt in your life to become successful. To be a good listener you should face the speaker and maintain your eye contact with him / her, be attentive and relaxed in your listening approach, keep silence, show interest, keep your mind open and listen the words of speaker properly and also don't interrupt him / her or change the subject at the time of speaking. In this way, you can include good qualities of a good listener in yourself. The listening skills are very important part of effective communication. It makes the speaker feel very connected to you, which help him / her to speak out without any hesitations. This skill provides you sense of better understanding to what another person is saying and thus you understand his case properly. When you don't understand any thing speaker / client is saying, in that case do not interrupt him / her, rather wait for right time to ask him to clarify the matter you did not understand and do not ask any unnecessary questions. Your questions should be restricted to ensure better understanding the topic / case only. You should also try to feel what the speaker is feeling, for that you require energy and concentration which can be developed by regular practice. You should also give the speaker / client regular feedback to his / her speaking by just nod and show your understanding through appropriate facial expression and an occasioned well time hmmm that means you give the speaker / client some proof that you are listening and you are following whatever is being speak. While talking face to face with your client you can also feel the enthusiasm, boredom or irritation of the speaker and better understand his / her mental status related to the topic being spoken. Thus it is very useful to develop your listening habits to be successful in your profession of advocacy.

Good speaker

The most important thing to become a successful lawyer is to be a good speaker. Here also you have to speak in presence of the public but speaking before the public in any program or occasion is quite different from speaking before the court for submitting your views before the court. One may be a very good public speaker outside the court room but may not be as efficient before the court, as before the public. Because there are so many ingredients, which requires, to be a good speaker, in a court of law, at the time of arguments. Speaking at events is a great way to enhance your PR for your business or profession. To become a great speaker is an art not a science. The good news is that with some tips and some practice you can acquire those speaking quality. You can leave a lasting impression before the people you want to be remembered. Here is some easy way that you can become a better speaker. Sometime we feel very connected and updated while listening any person. We also feel happy and feel like hearing the speaker as touched in some ways. The quality you experience is called charisma. Charisma is that special spiritual power or Personal qualities that gives an individual influence or authority over large number of people. A charismatic speaker leaves an impression on the audience large or small. Winston Churchill, Vivekanand, Mrs Indira Gandhi etc. are of such examples. To be a Charismatic speaker we have to learn the art of speaking. A charismatic speaker self confident and assured, they don't appear nervous or feel ease. They seem to be enjoying the speech and look energetic while speaking. When they speak it seems that their words are coming from his inner heart and also seem that they have the command over the topic over which they give speech. You can sense their emotions, enthusiasm and convictions very well. They are positive, cheerful cooperative and organised. Their points are clearly connected and logically follow one another with an overview at the beginning and a conclusion at the end. They are precise and complete. To be an honest, well mannered patient fair and responsible human being are also good track to become a good speaker and a good lawyer. By developing these qualities you too can be a charismatic speaker or a lawyer. By developing above written qualities, you will succeed with flying colour in the area of advocacy. Therefore speaking before the court you must care for all the discipline written above. Apart from that you require to understand the body language of the judges and their expectations from your side to make him understand the case in a better way. So at the time of your turn before the court you must be well acquainted with your cases and always should be in a position to reply the questions raised by the court. For replying in a better manner you required to have a better management of your file and for that you may take assistance of flagging system for your file, because it is always not possible to remember all the related facts of the case. So you have to adopt all those activities which are important to reply all the questions of the court within just a moment time. You may also make an index for your annexures and all likely questions to be asked by the court. For self preparation of the case you may also make questions and answer related to your case file, which is likely to be asked by the Honourable Court. Besides this you should make your eye contact to the people to whom you are speaking i.e. court here. It is also important for you to focus on a limited set of related ideas or facts and related Acts, so that it will not allow you to create a confusion regarding your case in the mind of judges. You should have gathered the quality for making the judges understand your case in a better way. You should also be careful about the clarity of your speech for making your case to understand in better way. You may also use some familiar examples of case already decided by the same court or some other courts. Please doesn't use one tone the entire speech, as it makes you your sound very dry dull and boring as a speaker and personality wise. It makes you a much better speaker when you raise your voice a bit here and there. Martin Luther King was one of the well known speaker in history his voice goes up and down and for getting a better speaking quality you may watch some videos of great speakers like Martin Luther King, John F Kennedy Mr Jawaharlal Nehru Mrs Indira Gandhi and Atal Bihari Vajpayee and by regular watching of the argument of renowned lawyer of your court is also helps you to organise your speech and speaking power in a positive direction as you also try to adopt the good quality of a lawyer. Apart from that your knowledge and reasoning capability is also increased which makes of a perfect speaker before the court of law. You may also use your hands while speaking. One must be very careful for not to put hands in the pocket because it seems to be a disregarding gesture in front of the Honourable Court. Putting hands to your pocket will do while you speak before the ordinary people's gathering but it will not do at all while you submitting your case before the court of law. So be careful and be alert in this regard. Speaking is one of the powerful skills to grow your business or profession and expand your opportunity to be successful in life. Good speaking increases your power of persuasion. When you become a good speaker you overcome fear of speaking. In this way you get rid of anxiety and nervousness while speaking before the public or judge in the courtroom. You develop confidence and power of attracting people / client. Your social connection is also developed and you acquire art of motivating others which ultimately result into your professional growth. There are many advantages to be a good speaker such as building credibility, building brand recognition, broadening marketplace reach, creating leads generation etc. to grow business or profession. Thus in this way we see that to become a successful person in legal profession you have to learn the speaking qualities of a successful lawyer which are described above.

Ways of Representation

This is also very important point for an advocate arguing a case before the court. Remember the judges sitting in the court are not a Lord or God. It is other point that some lawyer addresses him as Lordship. But he is also a man like you and me. So it is very important that don't hurt the ego of a judge. Second while representing before the court your ways that is your physical gesture, your language and your rhythm of speech is very important. Suppose you are representing an accused before the trial court then your way of Representation may be different at different occasion as per the need of the time. At the time of cross examination your ways of Representation will be different from your argument stage. Even your ways of argument will be different when a time comes when the judge pronounce punishment. These all matters are things to be learnt. Even at High Court and Supreme Court level you may easily differentiate ways of Representation which is different in different petitions argued by the lawyer.

While your appear for a case in which there is a violation of fundamental rights or other legal rights your force of speaking is different than a case where you represent your client in any appeal or in any bail matter. It is also very important to learn how successful lawyers argue a case of special leave petition and also have to learn your ways of argument in review, curative or a mercy petition before the Supreme Court of India, although it is not heard in open court and you have to submit your argument, if any, in written form. It can very easily be learn by a lawyer even free of cost by viewing the court

proceeding at the time when the eminent lawyer
makes his argument or do his work in his case.

Monetary Alertness

The monetary alertness is very important to come in the que of a successful lawyer. Because, in our society, money is an important yardstick to judge a successful person in the society. So you should also be very alert for earning money. The society has perception a good lawyer means big house big car etc. which is not always correct but in majority of cases the people starts thinking those people successful, having money. To have alertness for money does not mean that you should avoid the poor who comes to you for justice. It does not mean that if they are not capable to pay you more than you should not fight for them. But it means to say that those people capable of paying you should not be spared and you should charge him for your service as per his standard and paying capacity. If they are capable to pay you more, you should not charge less. Sometime even a rich man also try to avoid you to pay and even try to pay you less, in that case you must be very alert and tactful in your profession so that they may not take undue advantages from you. Become an Advocate from day one When you start your profession by enrolling yourself to the bar council, then you start to consider yourself as an advocate from the day one because, this will help you very much, in your professional career. You should visit the court everyday, wear your well dressed uniform in the court premises and also keep your visiting card with you. I am telling you this very small thing because there are so many advocates who are hesitant or reluctant to wear his / her uniform in the initial stages of his / her profession. Sometime they feel shy and so avoid wearing it. They are also not regular to the court because, in the initial time they do not have any work. So my advice is that if you do not have any work no problem, you visit the court, watch the proceeding, meet with other lawyers of your fraternity, study in the library etc. These all activities will give you knowledge confidence and recognition in a court you are practicing.

Don't run for or run after the clients

One of the very important suggestions for you, is that not to run for and run after your client. Here there are two different meaning for run for and run after the client. The meaning of run for the client means for getting a client one move to the prospective client to get a brief. It is not only illegal under advocates act but it also hampers dignity of a lawyer. Although, it is an illegal act and against to the professional ethics, of a lawyer, but some lawyer adopt this practice also. Some time in a court premises it is seen that some lawyer ask to prospective client for getting brief. Sometime it is also seen that a lawyer's Agent go to its prospective client for getting a vakalatnama signed even without getting a professional fee, usually in case of motor accident matters. Sometime they approach them just after accident when a family is in grief sorrow and sometime they approach them at a Funeral pyre. It is hight of the ill morality of this profession, which degrade the profession and advocates dignity very sharply. This sort of likely activities for getting a brief called Run for the clients, which is hindrance in the professional development of an advocate. Likewise the Advocate should not run after the client. To run after client means to follow your client physically, telephonically or through any other means. To make it more clear let us take one example. Suppose a person comes to you for a legal advice on any matter. He ask your free and also agrees to come to you later on. Then in that matter my advice is that, you kindly don't contact him through any means if he is not contacting you. If he contact you himself then its ok, otherwise if you will contact him you are never going to get this client's case and your reputation will also be hampered.

Watch the Court Proceedings

Watching the court proceeding is of immense importance for a practicing lawyer and even more useful for the new entrant of this profession. It may be called as one of the best way of learning art of advocacy. It does not only teach you the way of representing different type of cases before the court, it also increases your knowledge of law on relevant subject. It also teaches you the way of cross examination of different sort of witnesses. By watching a court proceeding you not only learn but it opens the door of your earning. You will be surprised here to listen this but it is true because while you watch the court proceeding different other lawyers and litigants are also present in the court room. They also start recognizing you as an advocate and you also get a chance to come in contact with them which brings a brief or work for you. Sometime other advocates also need help of some advocate in his case. They can also hire you for their professional work. Sometime even the court provides you the work by appointing you as a local commissioner or for some other work which also helps you for your professional and monetary development.

Avoid Close Intimacy

Being a law professional, as per my experience we should avoid close intimacy with any person for the professional development. In most of the examples of close intimacy, I felt that this intimacy itself is a barrier in the way of professional growth. Mind, your professional growth enhance from the brief you get from your client. A close intimacy in most of the time does not bring brief in your life. What that brings is advice by you free of cost to them. So my advice for a law professional is that you try to be an acquainted with more and more people of your society but do not develop the intimacy. Do not try to make them your fast friend. If you really want to search for your fast friend, then why not try in your own profession itself because it will not hamper your success. Rather it will help you more and more in your professional development, because you share your Idea you share the law points which helps you to understand your case, you are handling in a wide spread manner. I have also realized that a person having close intimacy to you will not give you much weightage as a professional. They underestimate you every time.

Even if he has any legal work he may ask you suggesting a good lawyer for them. Why they ask this because he feel you are not capable of handling their case. So dear friends, my most important advice to you, that, you say, goodbye to close intimacy with the person of the society.

Avoid tea coffee and other edibles

You're eating habits, in public and with your client and colleagues, also play a very important role in making your personality. My first advice regarding this is that kindly do not take any tea coffee and other edibles from your client side. Even if they offer you and you are compelled to a accompany them then not to forget to pay the bill from your own pocket. That will create a very positive personality in your self and the trust of the clients in you will also increase. I can say you by my personal experience that a client do not want to pay you more or sometime has no capacity to pay you more, they start influencing you by offering these products and by taking these all your mouth is even shut for demanding your professional fee from them, as you sometime feel obliged to them. Not only with your clients, I will say you should avoid taking these from your colleagues also. But it is no harm to join your colleagues in tea coffee and edibles but remember you should try to pay the bill first. These are the small things but counts very much in your professional life. Likewise your eating habits in public can also make or mar your personality. You should be very careful regarding your restricted eating habits. If you want to eat anything you can do it at your own house which will not affect your personality and reputation. So for creating a good personality track my advice is that your eating habit should be restricted and your manner should be decent

CHAPTER TWO

Essential Legal Skills

2.Essential Legal Skills

" If we desire respect for the law, we must first make the law respectful". – Louice D. Brandeis

Understand Case and its Jurisdiction

When a client comes to you with Case / brief, it is very important to understand the case and for that you have to listen the case very attentively and have to come to the conclusion as per the interest of your client. You require understanding the jurisdiction of the case, and where and in which Forum / Court you have to file the case. For understanding this you may get support from the concerned Act in which you are going to deal. Suppose you have to file a case for any defective goods, purchased by your client. Then you have to understand the case and its jurisdiction and for this the consumer protection act may help you a lot which can make you clear what type of case you can make and where to file your petition, within which time limit you have to file your petition etc. If suppose some other clients comes to you with his grievance which is related to his legal and fundamental rights then you have to understand the case of your client and make your effort in such a direction that his legal or fundamental rights may be restored. In that case you have to understand the provision of law as provided under article 32 and article 226, constitution of India so that you may file your case in a right direction. You have to understand, there are various types of Courts and Tribunals in India working for adjudication of justice. There is a Civil Court and Criminal court at district level and consumer forum Juvenile court at district level high court at state level and finally Supreme Court at the top. Apart from these courts there are so many tribunals in India. Railway tribunals, Central Administrative tribunals, Debt recovery tribunals, Education tribunals etc. So as per the case and the related act applied on the case you have to decide very carefully the jurisdiction for appropriate place for filing your case.

Drafting

Drafting is most important part of advocacy it is that part, on which entire case of your client depends. Drafting at the initial stage plays a very vital role, because only on this drafting the case pursued in further higher courts like Session court, High Court and Supreme Court. Therefore before drafting you must take care of following things. i) Facts of the case ii) Basic law related to your drafting iii) Relevant judgement of Supreme Court and high court related to the law for which you are going to draft your case. i)Facts of the case You must be very clear about the facts of your case. While drafting all facts, you just realise weather those facts are going to help your client as per his / her requirement and prayer of the petition. If it is not, then you should avoid writing those things and you should not make your petition bulky unnecessarily. While drafting petition, you should draw it in a chronological event of your case.

You should also try to arrange your annexures chronologically. That style of drafting gives a very clear cut understanding of the case. ii) Basic law related to your drafting Before drafting of your case you must consult the basic law related to your case, you are going to draft. Like law related to jurisdiction, limitation and other aspect of the law you are going to deal for this purpose you required to get basic knowledge of the law. So that you can draft your case as per requirement of the law. For this purpose you do not require a deep research on the matter, rather, your purpose may be solved by going through the bare acts related to the case. You have to go through the provision of CPC and CRPC along with rules of the High Court and Supreme Court regarding drafting, because the insertion of those directed points are very essential. You have to incorporate in your petition those points while drafting. We can take some example for clarifying these points of view. As for example, if you draft a petition for guardianship of a minor and her property, for that you have to go through the Bare Act of Guardian and wards act 1890 for the purpose of your drafting. First go through the index portion of the bare act, which will give you basic understanding that which section will help you for drafting and inserting those points in your petition. While reading the bear act in the present example, you will find section 10 of the guardian and ward act 1890 gives you direction for drafting your petition. Therefore you go through this section very carefully twice or thrice, for your better understanding. Section 10- Form of application (1) if the application is made by the collector, it shall be by petition sign and verified in manner prescribed by the code of civil procedure, 1882 (14 of 1882)1, for the signing and verification of a plaint, and stating, so far as can be ascertained,- a) the name, sex, religion, date of birth and ordinary residence of the minor. b) where the minor is a female, whether she is married and if so, the name and age of her husband. c)the nature situation and approximate value of the property, if any of the minor. d) the name and residence of the person having the custody or possession of the person or property of the minor. e) what near relations, the minor has and where they reside. f)whether a Guardian of the person or property or both, of the minor has been appointed by any person entitled or claiming to be entitled by the law to which minor is subject to make such an appointment. g) weather an application has at any time been made to the court or to any other court with respect to the guardianship of the person or property or both, of the minor and if so, when, to what court and with what result. h) whether the application is for the appointment or declaration of a guardianship of the person of the minor, or his property or both. i) where the application is to appoint a guardian, the qualification of the proposed guardian. j)where the application is to declare a person to be a guardian, the grounds on which that person claims, k) the causes which have led to the making of the application and l)such other particulars, if any, as may be prescribed or as the nature of the application renders it necessary to state. (2) If the application is made by the collector, it shall be by letter address to the court and forwarded by the post or in such other manner as may be found convenient, and shall state as far as possible the particulars mentioned in sub-section (1) (3) The application must be accompanied by a declaration of the willingness of the proposed guardian to act and the declaration must be signed by him and attested by at least two witnesses.

Thus by going through the section 10 of the Guardian and Wards Act 1890, it becomes very clear that what should be the contents of your petition / application, you are going to draft for this matter. We can understand this by taking some other example also. Suppose someone (a Hindu person) wants to file a petition for restitution of conjugal right or for divorce then for drafting your petition you have to go through the relevant sections of the Hindu Marriage Act 1955.

I am first taking restitution of conjugal rights which is there in under section 9 of the Hindu Marriage Act 1955. Section 9 :- Restitution of conjugal rights :- When either the husband or the wife has without reasonable cause, withdrawn from the society of the other, the aggrieved party may apply, by petition to the district court, for restitution of conjugal right and the court on being satisfied of the truth of the statements made in such petition and that there is no legal ground why the application should not be granted, may degree restitution of conjugal rights accordingly. Explanation - Where a question arises whether there has been reasonable excuse for withdrawal from the society, the burden of proving reasonable excuse shall be on the person who has withdrawn from the society.

Thus by reading this section 9, we have to look the provision which will help us drafting a petition / application for restitution of conjugal rights. We have to mention those facts in our application that the respondent withdrawn from the society of the applicant without any reasonable cause in this drafting. You have also, to go through the Family Court Act 1984, which provides jurisdiction to the family court for entertaining application, where family court is established, and not to the district court.

Likewise while drafting a petition of divorce under Hindu Marriage Act 1955; you have to go through section 13 of the Hindu Marriage Act 1955 which describes about the divorce. Section 13 divorce:- 1) any marriage solemnised, weather before or after the commencement of the Act, may on a petition presented by either the husband or the wife, be dissolved by a decree of divorce on the ground that the other party (i) has after the solemnization of the marriage, treated the petitioner with cruelty, or (ia)has deserted the petitioner for a continuous period of not less than two years immediately preceding the presentation of the petition, or (ii)has ceased to be a Hindu by conversion to another religion, or (iii) has been incurably of unsound mind, or has suffering continuously or intermittently from mental disorder of such a kind and two such an extent that the petitioner cannot reasonably be expected to live with the respondent. Explanation- In this clause- (a) the expression "mental disorder" means mental illness, arrested or incomplete development of mind, "psychopathic disorder" or any other disorder or disability of mind and include schizophrenia. (b) the expression "psychopathic disorder" means a persistent disorder or disability of mind (whether or not including sub-normality of Intelligence) which results in abnormally aggressive or seriously irresponsible conduct on the part of the other party and whether or not it requires or is susceptible to medical treatment, or (iv) has been suffering from a virulent and incurable form of leprosy, or (v) has been suffering from venereal disease in a communicable form, or (vi) has renounce the world by entering any religious order or (vii) has not been heard of as being alive for a period of seven years or more by those person who would naturally have heard of it, had that party been alive. Explanation :- In this sub-section the expression "desertion" means the desertion of the petitioner by the other party to the marriage without reasonable cause and without the consent or against the wish of such party, and includes the wilful neglect of the petitioner by the other party to the marriage, and its grammatical variation and cognate expression shall be construed accordingly. (1-A) Either party to marriage, weather solemnised before or after the commencement of this act may also present a petition for the dissolution of the marriage by a degree of divorce on the ground – (i) that there has been no resumption of cohabitation as between the parties to the marriage for a period of one year or upward after passing a degree of judicial separation in a proceeding to which they were parties; or (ii) that there has been no restitution of conjugal rights as between the parties to the marriage for a period of one year or upward after passing a degree of restitution of conjugal rights in a proceeding to which their were parties. (2) A wife may also present a petition for dissolution of her marriage by a degree of divorce on the ground- (i) in the case of any marriage solemnised before the commencement of this Act, that the husband had married again before the commencement or that any other wife of the husband married before such commencement was alive at the time of the solemnization of the marriage of the petitioner. provided that in either case the other wife is alive at the time of the presentation of the petition; (ii)That the husband has, since the solemnization of the marriage, been guilty of rape, sodomy or bestiality; or (iii) that in a suit under Section 18 of the Hindu Adoption and Maintenance Act (78 of 1956) or in a proceeding under section 125 of the code of criminal procedure 1973, (Act 2 of 1974), or under corresponding section 488 of the code of criminal procedure, 1898 (5 of 1898), a degree or order, as the case may be, has been passed against the husband awarding maintenance to the wife notwithstanding that she was living apart and that since the passing of such degree or order, cohabitation between the parties has not been resumed for one year or upward; or (iv) that her marriage (whether consummated or not) was solemnized before she attained the age of fifteen years and she has repudiated the marriage after attaining the age before attending the age of eighteen years. Explanation- This clause applies whether the marriage was solemnized before or after the commencement of the marriage law (Amendment) Act, 1976 (68 of 1976).

Thus by going through the section we come to know various things which is useful while drafting petition related to that case. We have to insert certain parts to our petition while drafting as per the requirement of law. In this way it is very important to go through related law on which you are going to draft your petition / application, so that your petition will not lack anything which is required as per the law. You have to insert those facts or law part as per statuary requirement. 3) Relevant judgement of Supreme court and high court related to law for which you are going to draught – The third important thing, before drafting you have to look is the judgement of the High court and Supreme court related to your case. We can understand this by taking example of dishonour of cheque case under section 138 of Negotiable Instrument Act 1881. If cheque is issued to you and if it is dishonoured, you have to issue a notice of dishonour to the issue of the cheque within reasonable time. Chapter VIII of N. I. Act 1881 describe about the notice of dishonour. Section under this from 91 - 98 describe about the various things regarding dishonour of cheque namely

91 - Dishonour by non- acceptance

92 - Dishonour by non payment

93 - By and to whom notice should be given

94 - Mode in which notice may be given

95 - Party receiving must transmit notice of dishonour

96 - Agent for presentment

97 - When party to whom notice given is dead

98 - When notice of dishonour is unnecessary

By looking these sections along with all other sections of Negotiable Instrument Act 1881, it may be noticed that there is nothing regarding the contents of the notice in specific section. There is only hint regarding this under section 94 i.e. mode in which notice may be given.

Section 94 - Mode in which notice may be given

Notice of dishonour may be given to duly authorised agent of the person to whom it is required to be given or where he has died to his legal representative or where he has been declared insolvent to his assignee, may be oral or written; may if written be sent by post; and maybe in any form but it must inform that the party to whom it is given; either in express terms or by reasonable intendment, that the instrument has been dishonoured; and in what way, and that he will be held liable thereon and it must be given within a reasonable time after dishonour, at the place of business or (In case such party has no place of business) at the residence of the party for whom it in is intended. If the notice is duly directed and sent by post and miscarriages such miscarriage does not render the notice invalid.

While drafting your legal notice for dishonour of cheque only to go through the relevant Bare Act of the case will not work, you have to go through the various judgement related to notice pronounced by the High Court and Supreme Court. In the judgement of the case of Suman Sathi versus Ajay Kumar Churawal & Anr. (2000) 2 SCC 380, K. R. Indira vs Dr. G. Adinarayana (2003) 8 SCC 301, Rahul builder vs Arihant fertilizers and Chemicals and Anr. (2008) 2 SCC 321, the apex court upon examining the above mentioned judgements held that, there is no question that the notice issued under section 138 of Negotiable Instrument Act 1881 has to be exclusive for the cheque amount. Therefore if your cheque amount and loan amount is different, that is loan amount is more, even then you have to demand the cheque amount only in your notice of dishonour otherwise your case may be dismissed by the magistrate citing above mentioned judgements of the supreme court. In other judgement i.e. Vijay Gopala Lohar vs. Pandurang Ramchandra gharpade & Anr. criminal appeal number 607608 / 2019, Supreme Court further clarified that the notice demanding Loan amount is not invalid if it is same as the cheque amount under 138 of Negotiable Instrument Act 1881. Therefore while drafting notice for dishonour of cheques, while demanding money you must demand for the cheque amount for the cheque which was dishonoured. Thus by going through this point, it becomes clear that for drafting you need not only to take the help of basic laws related to your case but also need to go through the relevant judgements of the High Court and Supreme Court. We can take some other example to understand this point more clearly. While drafting matrimonial case, the High Court of Delhi had ordered vide order dated 14ᵗʰ January 2015, this court formulated the affidavit of assets, income and expenditure to be filed by both the parties in matrimonial cases, in case of Kusum Sharma vs. Mahendra Kumar Sharma in FAO 297 / 1997.

This affidavit was again modified in Kusum Sharma vs. Mahendra Kumar Sharma FAO 369 / 1996 and

CM 15083 / 2014 by its judgement dated 29th may 2017. Thus in Delhi the parties to the matrimonial dispute, has to file the above written affidavit of assets income and expenditure which format is already inserted in the judgment itself. Therefore while filing a petition of matrimonial cases in Delhi the petitioner has to file a written affidavit along with the petition, otherwise the petition is not been taken for consideration. In this way we see that, we must have knowledge of relevant judgement for which we are going to draft our case.

Get Certified Copy of your Case File

Getting certified copy of your case file is also very important and helpful for a lawyer, as corruption is so rampant particularly in lower Judiciary that even the case file is managed and sometime papers of your support is lost even from the court file, as it is come to listen from time to time. In that time certified copy taken by you, helps you too much. Although, it cost you some money, but make your habit to take certified copy of your case file time to time.

Professional Attitude

To be a successful in any profession the professional attitude of a person is very important. Professional attitude is those quality and characters of any particular profession, which helps the person to work in a best possible manner for performing his work, in a dignified way. A lawyer has a duty, of course to do his very best for the clients. But there is no place in the profession for masochism and hardball tactics. He should be effective, and assertive in his argument. It is not mean that lawyer treat his opposition with contempt and discourtesy. The legal profession is a branch of administration of justice and a lawyer is officer of the court. It is not mere money getting occupation; rather it is called a "calling". In addition to service to the public and administration of justice courtesy and ethics are also important component of professionalism. A lawyer has a duty to respect his client vigorously but has no place for rudeness and discourtesy. He represents his clients before the court, but it does not mean that he is the mouthpiece of his client. It is absolute necessity that a lawyer representation for word be as good as gold, which can have a positive impact on the person to whom he speaks. The ethics of the profession are not the ethics of the market place. The value of honour and integrity must never be compromised by a lawyer. It is not necessary to be discourteous to throw your weight around, to be antagonistic, or to otherwise lack that degree of civility so essential in the conduct of human affairs. Fundamentally, a lawyer owes opposing Counsel honesty and candour, courtesy and cooperation. All this he owes to be the occupant of the bench as well. A lawyer unquestionably owes to the administration of justice, the fundamental duties of professional dignity and professional integrity. A client has no right to demand that, counsel abuse the opposite party or indulge in offensive conduct and even he should not do so. A lawyer shall always treat adverse witnesses and suitors with fairness and due consideration. The both opposing party may have ill feeling for each other but such ill feeling should not influence a lawyer's conduct, attitude or demeanour towards opposing lawyer or parties. A lawyer will be punctual in communications with others and in honouring schedule appearance, and will recognise the neglect and tardiness are demeaning to the lawyer and to the judicial system. A lawyer should not use any tactics with the sole motto of harassing the opposite party and their lawyers. If a fellow member of the bar makes a just request for cooperation or seek scheduling accommodation, a lawyer will not arbitrarily or unnecessary with hold consent. Effective advocacy does not require antagonistic or obnoxious behaviour and members of the bar will adhere to the higher standard of conduct which judges, lawyer, client and the public may rightfully expect. A lawyer must be ready to waive his own personal interest if the interests of his client are clashing with his own interest for the sake of administration of justice. If matter is being settled through compromise he should not delayed the case by indulging into unnecessary litigation. The profession of a law is not a short of business it is distinguished by the requirement of extensive formal training and learning, admission to practice by qualifying licensure, a code of ethics imposing standards. Lawyers are officers of the court but historical fact and by statutory law. We must again be brought around to the reality that a lawsuit is indeed a surch for truth and not one for our economic game. A professional must be well dress up. Your appearance is often the first thing that people judge you on: when you look like a professional you are more likely to be perceived as a professional. The attitude of professional is very positive and he has to

Prove his competency to the Client or people of the society. Part of being professional is getting the job done and doing it well. You should possess the skill that you need in order to do your job while also taking it upon yourself to improve in the area where you are deficient. These attitudes of professionals are highly welcomed. You reliability is also very important therefore proving that you are reliable can help you to present a professional attitude. Being a lawyer I suggest a good lawyer must have a call to his client before the date in the court so that he may come to the court in time to participate in the proceeding. If he does not come then he / she must be informed about the court proceedings. Apart from that a lawyer must reach the court before the time. All these attitude of a lawyer creates a belief of the confidence to his client, which pays a lot to professional like advocate. A good lawyer treats his co-worker or staff with respect and in a friendly manner. He / She also avoid gossiping and bad mouthing anyone, which is the fastest way to ruin your reputation.

AOR (Advocate On Record)

To be a successful in the profession, you may also opt for other fields like AOR i.e. Advocate on Record in Supreme Court. First to be an AOR is also a good opportunity for a lawyer, as it provides some extra benefits over the other lawyers. Being an AOR, you can not only argue your case before the Supreme Court of India but you can get right to file the case before this court. This is the exclusive right of an AOR. Not only filing the case before this court, the

Supreme court also provides advantages to an AOR in the chamber allotment. Out of ten chambers seven chambers are allotted to an AOR, two chambers or Non-AOR Advocate and one chamber for Senor Advocate, which is of great advantage.

For becoming an AOR, you have to take training under an advocate on record, having at least ten year of standing as an advocate on record and after completion of your training you have to appear in the examination conducted by the Supreme Court. After four years of experience as an advocate this training of one year is required. Before starting training under an advocate on record, you require a certificate of an advocate on record under whom you are going to take training, which required to be deposited in the registry of advocate on record section of the Supreme Court. And after completion of your training also, you require a certificate from an advocate on record under whom you have completed your training, which is again to be deposited in the registry. After this registry issue a certificate to the advocate and thus he / she become entitled to appear in the advocate on record examination. You get maximum five term to appear in the examination. In the syllabus of this examination, there are four papers of 100 marks each and you have to score at leat 60% marks in aggregate with 50 marks at leat to pass in a paper. The papers and its syllabus are being given here for your better understanding.

(I) Practice and Procedure of Supreme Court-

i) Relevant provisions in the constitution of India relating to the jurisdiction of the court.

ii)Supreme Court Rules and relevant provisions of civil procedure code, Limitation Act and the General Principles of Court Fee Act.

(II) Drafting- i) Petition for Special leave and Statement of case etc.

ii) Decree & orders and writs.

(III) Advocacy & Professional Ethics

(iv) Leading Cases- A list of leading cases are made available to the candidates at the time of notification of the Advocate on – Record Examination.

For further details regarding this examination, you may also contact concern registry of the Supreme Court, who may guide you properly.

Patent Agent

If you are a science or engineering graduate apart
from you Law Degree, you have one better option to
work as a Patent Agent. Although for appearing in the
examination of Patent Agent you need not require to
have a law degree. But being a lawyer from science or
engineering background, you have always extra
benefits over others. A patent agent is an individual
who is registered for practicing before an Indian
Patent Office. To become one, one has to qualify
Indian Patent Agent Exam that is held each year by
the Indian Patent Office once in a year. This
examination is conducted at Mumbai, Delhi, Nagpur,
Chennai and Kolkata. The applicant is to select a

centre of his convenience. The eligibility criteria to become patent agent India are as follows:

• Applicants need to be an Indian citizen and is to complete 21 years of age at exam time. • All technology and science graduates (M.Tech, B.Tech, M.Sc. and B.Sc,) from any established university under Indian law or other specified equivalent qualification under central government is eligible for appearing the exam.

• The final year candidates also are eligible on producing the mark sheets, final degree, etc., within two months from Patent Agent exam result.

• Indian Patent Office has not specified till date the maximum number of attempts to qualify this exam, which means one can appear as many times until he qualifies his / her patent agent examination. Even though there is no prescribed syllabus format as prescribed by Indian patent office, one has to become thorough with procedures and practice of patent office and should also have knowledge of Patent Act & Rules and drafting different specification etc. One should get hold of the latest and well researched study materials and be competent and well versed for clearing Patent Agent Exam. For better understanding the syllabus of this examination, you may download previous year question papers from the website of Patent office i.e. http://www.ipindia.nic.in

The certification after passing this exam is valid only

for India and recognized only by Indian patent office. Any individual desiring to practice outside the country like Europe or the US, needs to qualify patent agent exam of respective countries.

For desiring to appear in Patent agent examination you must be very vigilant and be in contact with Patent Office, as the exam gets announced by Patent Office, forms could be filled on the web through official website or could be downloaded, filled up and sent to the specified postal address. Therefore be in regular touch with the website as mentioned above, of patent office and also inquire telephonically from time to time for the examination.

Try to file PIL Cases

PIL means Public Interest Litigation. It is one of the most important tools in the hands of a lawyer to be successful in the profession. As it is very important for a lawyer to be social and be the part of the social activities going on in society. Filing PIL by a lawyer is nothing but his "Social Activism" through law. PIL is not defied in any statute. It is the outcome of a judicial activism to take cognisance of cause at the instance of any person even if, it does not affect him personally, but affects the public at large.

If you feel that due to lack of or misguided government policies, policies effecting fundamental rights of a persons of the society and any decisions of government are hampering the greater common good and creating unacceptable and undesirable situations related to abuse and violation of basic human rights, social injustice corruption etc society is effecting adversely, your brain is working in the right direction to file for appropriate direction to the government by filing a proper PIL before the High Court or Supreme Court. You must be very-very vigilant or aware citizen of your nation and must be very alert regarding governmental policies and work and its impact on the society. This attitude of alertness will provide you a good opportunity to file a PIL case. As PIL cases are very important to the society, therefore society is also very vigilant toward these sorts of cases. Thus if you are successful in filing PIL cases, then you become successful leaving your impact to the society at large and you are recognized by the society, as one of the good lawyer. It gives you name power also, which ultimately make you successful in the profession, because in our profession of advocacy name power counts much which brings briefs to you and through this briefs money also.

As a lawyer, a PIL should not be filed in haste. You must first try to redress your grievances to the concerned department of the government for proper redressal. If there is no action or proper reply, then study your case deeply and take assistance of some other lawyers also and decide whether your case is fit to be filed as a PIL case or not. There is supreme court guideline also regarding filing of the PIL cases. Therefore it is better to go through those guidelines and then take a decision to file a PIL; otherwise court may impose a heavy cost to you for filing a false and frivolous PIL.

Supreme Court of India guideline for PIL

COMPILATION OF GUIDELINES TO BE FOLLOWED FOR ENTERTAINING LETTERS/PETITIONS RECEIVED IN THIS COURT AS PUBLIC INTEREST LITIGATION. (Based on full Court decision dated 1.12.1988 and subsequent modifications). No petition involving individual/ personal matter shall be entertained as a PIL matter except as indicated hereinafter. Letter-petitions falling under the following categories alone will ordinarily be entertained as Public Interest Litigation:-

1. Bonded Labour matters.

2. Neglected Children.

3. Non-payment of minimum wages to workers and exploitation of casual workers and complaints of violation of Labour Laws (except in individual cases).

4. Petitions from jails complaining of harassment, for (pre-mature release)* and seeking release after having completed 14 years in jail, death in jail, transfer, release on personal bond, speedy trial as a fundamental right. *$ Petitions for premature release, parole etc. are not matters which deserve to be treated as petitions u/Article 32 as they can effectively be dealt with by the concerned High Court. To save time Registry may simultaneously call for remarks of the jail Superintendent and ask him to forward the same to High Court. The main petition may be forwarded to the concerned High Court for disposal in accordance with law. Even in regard to petitions containing allegations against Jail Authorities there is no reason why it cannot be dealt with by the High Court. But petitions complaining of torture, custody death and the like may be entertained by this Court directly if the allegations are of a serious nature.

(5) Petitions against police for refusing to register a case, harassment by police and death in police custody.

(6) Petitions against atrocities on women, in particular

harassment of bride, bride burning, rape, murder, kidnapping etc. + In such cases where office calls for police report if letter petitioner asks for copy the same may be supplied, only after obtaining permission of the Hon'ble Judge nominated by the Hon'ble Chief Justice of India for PIL matters. -------------------------- -- $ Added based on Order dated 19.8.1993 of the then Chief Justice of India.

(7) Petitions compplaining of harassment or torture of villagers by co- villagers or by police from persons belonging to Scheduled Caste and Scheduled Tribes and economically backward classes.

(8) Petitions pertaining to environmental pollution, disturbance of ecological balance, drugs, food adulteration, maintenance of heritage and culture, antiques, forest and wild life and other matters of public importance.

(9) Petitions from riot -victims.

(10) Family Pension.

All letter-petitions received in the PIL Cell will first be screened in the Cell and only such petitions as are covered by the above mentioned categories will be placed before a Judge to be nominated by Hon'ble the Chief Justice of India for directions after which the case will be listed before the Bench concerned. If a letter-petition is to be lodged, the orders to that effect

should be passed by Registrar (Judicial) (or any Registrar nominated by the Hon'ble Chief Justice of India), instead of Additional Registrar, or any junior officer. To begin with only one Hon'ble Judge may be assigned this work and number increased to two or three later depending on the workload. *Submission Notes be put up before an Hon'ble Judge nominated for such periods as may be decided by the Hon'ble Chief Justice of India from time to time. **If on scrutiny of a letter petition, it is found that the same is not covered under the PIL guidelines and no public interest is involved, then the same may be lodged only after the approval from the Registrar nominated by the Hon'ble the Chief Justice of India. **It may be worthwhile to require an affidavit to be filed in support of the statements contained in the petition whenever it is not too onerous a requirement. ----------
----

- + Added as per Order dated 29.8.2003 of the Hon'ble Chief Justice of India. * As per Order dated 29.8.2003 of the Hon'ble the Chief Justice ofIndia. **The matters which can be dealt with by the High Court or any other authority may be sent to them without any comment whatsoever instead of all such matters being heard judicially in this Court only. Cases falling under the following categories will not be entertained as Public Interest Litigation and these may be returned to the petitioners or filed in the PIL Cell, as the case may be: (1) Landlord-Tenant matters. (2) Service matter and those pertaining to Pension and Gratuity. (3) Complaints against Central/ State Government Departments and Local Bodies except those relating to item Nos. (1) to (10) above. (4) Admission to medical and other educational institution. (5) Petitions for early hearing of cases pending in High Courts and Subordinate Courts. In regard to the petitions concerning maintenance of wife, children and parents, the petitioners may be asked to file a Petition under sec. 125 of Cr. P.C. Or a Suit in the Court of competent jurisdiction and for that purpose to approach the nearest Legal Aid Committee for legal aid and advice.

** Modified keeping in view the directions dated 29.8.2003 of the Hon'ble Chief Justice of India

CHAPTER THREE

Develop and Maintain Contacts

"The richest people in the world build networks. Everyone else look for work" – Robert Kiyosaki

Five persons per day Rule

I advise you to make a routine work to contact at least five persons per day, through your personal physical meetings or through telephone or any other means like social media. This will help you to increase in your contacts list as well as for revival of your contacts. For that you may congratulate your contacts and wish them as per their occasions. Some time you may send email or letter by post for wishing some special occasions. You may also ask their opinions regarding any issue. You may also send them a particular links to your contacts which may be useful to them, as per their business or liking. It would be better if you can maintain a list of your contacts. For maintaining and developing your contacts you should be very vigil to the liking and disliking of your contacts. Appreciations to others also play a very important role in developing and maintaining your contacts. You should be also very mindful in knowing the limitations. Never indulge in gossiping as you have to develop your professional contacts. Remember you must trust them and respect them and full fill your word, if any given by you to them. In this way you may create a network which may be useful for your profession. This may also be useful for exchange of information, advice and referrals for your profession. In this way it will assists you for attending your goal.

Try to build a long-term relationship and good reputation. You try to meet people who can assist you and potentially help you in return. If you are going to any programme where you are suppose to meet new people, and then you plan ahead and have some relevant points of discussion in your mind. It may not relate only to work but also be related to the topic like hobbies or the event itself. While developing contacts your motto of conversation should be to leave room for future meetings and discussions so that you can meet and talk them to provide your contacts some bounding. The connections strength your profession and also give you some fresh idea to develop your profession. It also builds your knowledge power and self confidence as you also develop interconnected business / professional contacts.

ARC Triangle

ARC Triangles means Affinity, Reality and Communication Triangle. L. Ron Hubbard, author of the #1 New York Times Bestseller Dianetics, describe about this triangle in his book "Scientology a new Slant on Life". The ability to use this triangle gives a much greater understanding of life, as this ARC triangle is the key stone of living associations

1) Affinity- The first corner of the triangle is called affinity which means "love, liking or any other emotional attitude which can also be understood by "degree of liking". Under affinity we have the various emotional tones which are represented below.

Serenity The Highest Level Enthusiasm Conservatism

Boredom

Antagonism

Anger

Covert Hostility

Fear

Grief

Apathy The Lowest Level

As we proceed from up to down there is lesser affinities.

Fig:- Tone Scale

Affinity is conceived to be comprised first of thought, then of emotion.

2) Reality:- It is the second corner of a triangle which could be defined as "that which appears to be". It may be considered as the Agreement i.e. the point where we as a human being agree may be called Reality.

3) Communication:- This is considered as the third corner of ARC Triangle. Communication is considered as most important thing in this triangle to understand the composition of human relations. The

point has to be understand in this triangle is

a) Without a high degree of liking (affinity) and without some basis of agreement i.e. Reality there is no communication.

b) Without communication and some basis of emotional response (affinity) there can not have reality (agreement).

c) Without some basis for agreement and communication there will be no affinity. We call these three things as triangle. Unless we have two corner of ARC triangle, we can not have its third corner and for describing any corner of it, one must describe other two corners also. This triangle is not consisted of all equal sides. Affinity and Reality is very much, less important then communication, as it begins with communication and brings affinity and reality.

So you simply understand while develop your contacts, your communication is very-very important. Because if your communication is good then you can also attract affinity and reality described above. All the three things are important for greater understanding and for living life more meaningful. If you have no affinity at all, you can not try to communicate with others and there will be no reality (agreement). If there is no reality, you will not have affinity and you will also not try to communicate. In this way while understanding and developing your contacts, you have to see all the three things in other person also. If they have one, you can supplant other two and can develop your relationship. For example if any one try to talk with you then you can also take interest and try to talk with them and surch out his thoughts and emotions (i.e. affinity) and reality (i.e. agreement) and talk on the line, then you have a better understanding with the person. Likewise if you feel other persons love, like and other emotional attitudes, you can try to communicate on that line, you will have a common agreement which will also help you to develop better relationship. In the same manner if there is some common agreement (reality) between you and other person, you can start communicate, and then affinity will also develop. In this way we see the communication is the biggest tool for developing relationship and for a healthier relationship all the three corner of a triangle is must. This technique can be used to talk unknown persons also to develop your relationship.

Attending functions and seminars

For a lawyer it is always beneficial to attend different functions and seminars from where they are called to be attended. When you go to attend those functions and seminars you come across different other people who may be your prospective clients. When you attend these sort of function, you also try to be a speaker, if there is an opportunity for you to speak, because being a speaker you come in contact with many people in a short duration and the people also starts recognizing you. When you are recognized by some person then it also gives you an opportunity to come in contact with some other unknown people. In this way your network of acquainted people will increased. Remember when you attend any such programme you must not forget to mingle with the people and you should also keep your visiting card in your pocket so that you may exchange your contacts also. You can also take interest in those peoples and try to take their visiting cards and if card is not there with them, then you may take their phone or mobile number, so that you mar contact them in future. Attending these sort of programme not only increase your circle of acquintants but it also develop your professional knowledge because if you are being called as an speaker, then you have to prepare yourself to speak before the audiences and if you are being called as listener, even then you get knowledge from other speakers. It also gives you an idea of good speaking and its ways. In this way it is an opportunity for you to convert yourself as a good speaker which is one of the most important factors to be a successful lawyer.

Try to Organize Seminars

To organize seminars is also a good step in becoming a successful lawyer. Because you know that lawyers profession is mostly depends on two things viz, contacts and knowledge. In organizing seminars you get both of them, good numbers of new contacts as well as knowledge. For this you first select the topic of the seminar and after selecting it you try to study on this topic so that you can organize your programme very well. This will enhance your knowledge on the topic. After that you try to contact different speakers from the society. For selecting your speakers even you can go beyond your contacts, you can talk and meet new peoples also. You can also meet people for arranging place for your seminar. Some time you also contact people for taking donations for your function. You also contact people to invite in your function. Hear it is worth mentioning that for this programme you may invite participants through social media like Facebook, twitter, instagram, whatsapp ect. As through inviting from social media you may get large number of participant and mostly they will be new for you. Likewise attending seminars and other functions, will also helps you in increasing you constats and knowledge. But do not forget to keep your visiting card in some extra in number so that you may share your cards to other participants or persons. While attending / arranging / organizing seminar you come in contact with large number of people some of them may be known to you and some other may be new, which increases your network. In this way it helps you not only developing your contacts but for reviving and maintaining your contacts also.

Handling cases of your relations and close friends

It is most difficult client handling situations. Firstly most of you relations who comes to you for any legal help will ask you a better lawyer for his case, because they underestimate you. It is another matter that you may be one of the best lawyers of that court. Sometime if they want service from you, they do that by considering you will charge fewer fees or nil from them. In these situations you need to understand the psychology of client who in your relation and close friends. If you are not very much able to understand then it is my advice that do not handle their cases alone rather take the help of some other lawyer and tell then for contesting their case in more effective way you need the help of some other lawyer for expert advice and in this way you will also be free to charge the professional fee as per you demand as you are taking professional help from some other lawyer. The great advantage of hiring some other lawyer is that your relation / close friend client would not be able to blame you directly in any odd situation. You will be in a position to tell you that as per the need he took the help of some other expert lawyer also.

Politics and a Lawyer

To be in the politics for a lawyer is very beneficial from professional point of view, because the success mantra for a lawyer largely depends on networking. The politics gives a better platform to develop contacts through working for peoples of the society and raise the voice on behalf of public at large. Therefore I feel an advocate should also involve himself in this activity so that he can develop large number of contacts which may ultimately turn into professional benefits. For this activity a lawyer can involve himself in different elections of the bar associations. Beside this he may also involve in the election of the Society, NGO, Trust, Residents Welfare Association, Counselors, and Member of Legislative Assembly and also for Member of Parliament. Contesting elections of the Bar, not only gives you recognition among your colleague brothers and sisters, whether you win an election or not. But when you win the election you also become the member of decision making committee of Bar Association. You get various opportunity to take part in different meetings with different sort of peoples which again increases your contacts. You also get an opportunity to meet with judges which increase your value as it is called "face value" in front of judges, because judges also stars recognizing you. In this way you get more attention by your clients. Apart from that being a member of executive committee of Bar Association, you get opportunity to meet persons of different department of government, which may help also you at the time of applying for the Panel of various governmental department, as you can establish relationship with those persons. You may also contest the election for counsellor, MLA or MP. In that case many peoples stars recognizing you and they also come to know that you are an advocate by profession. In this way your marketing for your advocacy also takes place indirectly, which is otherwise not allowed by the rule of Bar Council of India to advertise for your profession. It results into more contacts, more clients and more earning. One can join a political party of his / her own choice, work on the problem of the local area, raise voice on the issues and even to file PIL cases related to problems are such political activity which provide a lawyer a large base area for his own network development and recognition in the society. You not only come into contact with persons of the society but with the cadres of that very political party which ultimately gives you opportunity to serve them legally at the time of requirements. In India for joining politics there is no prerequisite qualification, but lawyer class here is most successful class to grow in politics. Most of the top leaders in any political party are occupied by lawyers or with person having law decree. A lawyer's work is of such type that you work for politics but can reap benefits in lawyering and even you work as a lawyer you can reap benefits as a politician. Therefore the benefits in these two professions are complementary to each other. In this way a political activities or career is of extra advantage for a lawyer. A politics gives a lawyer, a platform to interact the peoples in the name of developing his / her political party in the locality or given area of responsibility. Therefore at the time of developing party, a lawyer also develop his network, from where prospective client will come. Without joining any political party or a social organization, it is very difficult for a lawyer to interact with the people of the society. Therefore it is a gateway of interacting people of the society and be successful in the profession.

Art of influencing people

The personality of influencing people is one of the positive characters of a person. In advocacy also, it plays a great role. After all to be successful in this profession one of the important mantras is your contacts, contacts and your contacts. So if you are well versed in the art of influencing people, you are certainly going to increase your friends list and they become your prospective client. For developing these character in better way, you may go through the book of Dale Carnegie`s "How to Win Friends and Influence People", who described art of influencing people in a very good manner, which also helps you to develop your overall personality. But in short for getting this trait some most important point from the book is reproduced as below.

1. Don'nt criticize, condemn or complain any one.

2. Give honest and sincere appreciation.

3. Arouse in other person an eager want.

4. Be a good listener, encourage others to talk about themselves.

5. Talk in terms of other person's interests.

6. Make the other person feel important and do it sincerely.

7. Become genuinely interested in other people

8. Smile

9. Call the person by his / her name. Remember person name is to that person the sweetest and most important sound in any language.

10. Avoided any sort of argument with any people.

11. Respect the opinion of other person.

12. Never say you are wrong to any person.

13. If you are wrong, admit it without any delay.

14. Start any thing in a friendly manner.

15. Respond the other person saying yes-yes where required.

16. Allow other person to talk with you.

17. Appreciate persons effort make them feel that it is his idea, which is great.

18. Try to se the things from other's point of view.

19. Respect others idea or desire.

20. Stand by or appeal to the novel motives.

21. Dramatize your ideas.

22. Throw down a challenge.

23. Begin with praise and honest appreciation.

24. In out the peoples mistake in indirect way.

25. Don't criticise other, rather talk about your own mistake first then point to others.

26. Don't give any one order, rather ask question for help

27. Let the other person save face.

28. Be "hearty in your appreciation and lavish in your praise." For that praise the slightest improvement and praise every improvement.

29. Give the other person a file reputation to live up

to.

30. Make the fault seem easy to correct for that encourage other person.

31. Make other people happy, doing the thing you have suggested.

All these points are very well described by the writer of the book. These all qualities will help you more outside the court room. Inside the court room or before the judges you have to be very choosy among them which suit you as per the requirement of time.
But certainly these qualities written above will increase your friends and network, which is the prime thing for your profession.

CHAPTER FOUR

Continuous Legal Education

4.Continuous Legal Education

"Formal education will make you a living; self education will make you a fortune" – Jim Rohn

Legal Education

For a lawyer education never ends. It should be continued till the end of your profession. Here education does not mean only the prescribed degree but it apply for education, even you are not getting any degree but knowledge wise you develop yourself gradually. But along with your profession if you acquire knowledge along with some other degree in law, is of great importance for you as you get yourself recognized degree wise also. Although for practicing law LLB degree in law is sufficient. So any how your continuous legal education should not be stopped, whether you get recognized degree by doing so. To be continuous in legal profession, continue your legal education by making your daily habit of going through the legal books and journal and daily newspaper etc which make you abreast with the latest development in the field of law. Apart from that you should also attend seminars and study circles organized by bar council, bar associations and other organizations. Some time it is also very useful to make a group of lawyer and start your own study circles by inviting some eminent lawyer of a particular field to deliver speech on the subject. It does not only make you knowledgeable but also brings you contact with the eminent legal luminaries from whom you can learn a lot. They may also guide you when you require any help for your legal work.

Habits of studying leading cases

To study leading cases is very important for a practicing lawyer, because it opens the mind of lawyers for skilled advocacy. It not only helps you in your case at the time of argument but it also increases your thought process which helps you very much to present your views/ points on behalf of your clients. For reading leading cases you must start from its origin. You have to be very careful while studying, whether the case starts from the trial court or from High Court or from Supreme Court itself. This makes you to understand the case in a better way. You should also categorize the different leading cases into different-different class e.g. while studying cases related to basic structure of the constitution, you have to make one segment of all the cases related to the basic structure of our constitution. The basic structure of the constitution was propounded in Kesavananda Bharati v. State of Kerala (case citation: AIR 1973 SC

1461) case. Then your reading patter of studying leading case will start before the Kesavananda Bharati case where related matter was discussed to see its origin. You have to start from Shankari Prasad Singh Deo v. Union of India (AIR. 1951 SC 458), and Sajjan Singh v. State of Rajasthan (case citation: 1965 AIR 845, 1965 SCR (1) 933), In both cases, the power to amend the rights had been upheld on the basis of Article 368. In I.C. Golak Nath and Ors. vs. State of Punjab and Anr. The Court held that an amendment of the Constitution is a legislative process, and that an amendment under article 368 is "law" within the meaning of article 13 of the Constitution and therefore, if an amendment "takes away or abridges" a Fundamental Right conferred by Part III, it is void. You should also study the post Kesavananda Bharati case where the basic structure of the constitution was discussed or reaffirmed e,g. I. R. Coelho (deceased) by LRS. v. State of TamilNadu 2007 (2) SCC 1: 2007 AIR(SC) 861 case where the basic structure of the constitution was discussed and reaffirmed the Kesavananda Bharati case. Likewise you may categorize leading cases base on different other topics e.g. cases related to the reservation where you have to go through the various case like State of Madras v. Champakam Dorairajan AIR 1951 SC 226, M. R. Balaji v. State of Mysore AIR 1963 SC 649, Syndicate Bank SC & ST Employees Association & Others v. Union of India & Others 1990 SCR(3) 713; 1990 SCC Supl. 350, Indira Sawhney & Others v. Union of India AIR 1993 SC 477, General Manager Southern Railway v. Rangachari AIR 1962 SC 36,

State of Punjab v. Hiralal 1970(3) SCC 567, Akhil Bharatiya Soshit Karamchari Sangh (Railway) v. Union of India (1981) 1 SCC 246, Union of India v. Varpal Singh AIR 1996 SC 448, Ajitsingh Januja & Others v. State of Punjab AIR 1996 SC 1189, M. Nagraj & Others v. Union of India and Others.AIR 2007 SC 71, Ashoka Kumar Thakur v. Union of India 2007 RD-SC 609 etc. In this way you have to categorize different leading cases and will have to make comparative study of the judgments.

Habit of studying legal journals, Blogging, writing articles and books etc.

These qualities of studying legal journals, blogging, writing articles and books are also very important to be successful in profession of law. By doing so, it gives you an intellectual outlook and it is also a way to reveal your inner potential in front of the public at large, who might be your prospective clients. Your positive image is also starts building by doing so. It is an era of internet. So many peoples are available on internet and also require help to surch the solution of their problems. Blogging gives you a strong online influence, develop your writing skills, as more you blog, more you write, and better writer / blogger you become. When you publish your article in depth in you blog related to any legal issues, it helps the people to solve their problem by going through your blog. They start trust you, respect you and consider you as an expert in your field of work and if they want more help then a blog post can offer, they would certainly like to contact you and take your services. Sometime blogging itself become part of your earning which develop you financially also which ultimately boost your legal career. In blogging you get feedback also from its readers which also help to develop your writing skills, analyse your influencing power and your reputation. Blogging also helps you to take control of your online identity, build trust among the people, and increase your power of expression as it is powerful form of expression. It also helps other people to get solutions of their problem. The habit of regular blogging helps you studying different skills and knowledge so that you may hoist a new blog. In this way you become more knowledgeable in your field. When you write a series of in-depth valuable articles related to your profession, Google / internet also takes notice. Therefore it is an opportunity to you to get traffic from search and thus it improves your SEO. Blogging also increases your network. If your blog is valuable and interesting it will certainly attract readers who may comment on your site. They may send you personal massages also and can also ask for the help. Some of the readers may help you also. Thus it increases your networking circle which ultimately results in success to your profession. The most important point which one can not ignore, that the blogging gives you the status of a published author. In the same way by writing articles for news paper or magazine or by publishing your own book you get all those benefits described above while discussing about blogging. Doing all these work is not very tough but very easy for a professional. So I will advice you write on that very topic on which you are working as a professional, because while working for you clients, you have to go through different books and journals. So you convert your this labour for blogging, writing articles and books. You will certainly feel how easy you have written all that and established yourself as a writer. As an established writer, it brings you name and fame which attract money also. Thus you become a successful man of your area.

CHAPTER FIVE

Managerial and understanding capabilities

5.Managerial and understanding capabilities
"Management is above all, a practice where art, science and craft meet" – Henry Mintzberg

Brief not only a case but an opportunity

When any brief comes to you for litigation, it is not only a case but is a good opportunity to show your talent for providing relief to the clients. Remember there is an old slogan "money begets money" and I tell you "clients beget clients and client begets money also. So if any case comes to you, you must be very sincere and focused to the relief, your clients want in the interest of justice. If any brief comes to you, your most important work is to consult the books on relevant laws and firstly try to find out its jurisdiction, because filing a case before a competent authority is the prime factor and fate of the case largely depends upon it. If you file a case in wrong jurisdiction your case can be struck down at initial stage itself. So deciding the jurisdiction and choosing the court for filing case is very-very important. There will be various cases where you have to select appropriate court for your relief because there are many cases which may be file in District civil court and the High court also due to its nature. In that case you have to select the court very carefully as per the facts and circumstances of your case. So you tackle your case very sincerely and make your full efforts, can easily be accessed by your client which ultimately results into the recommendation for you by your client to other people and I tell you the recommendation by your client to other people for you gives much more positive result for your professional development. You also must remember that the clients interest is most important and when there is a clash between clients interest and advocates own interest, a good advocate should forget his own interest and sacrifice this over the interest of you client and do best for his client. Advocate should not consider that the case is his last case and not be inclined to earn money only over the interest of the client, because if he will think so then there will be a lot of delay in deciding the case of his client, which may shatter the faith of the client in judiciary. Therefore a lawyer must try to finish the case of his client as soon as possible in the best interest of his client. It is also seen sometime that delaying tactic of a lawyer also helps his client and they also feel good to delay the case. In that situation a successful lawyer try to delay the matter by filing different sort of application before the court by finding the loopholes in the pleadings of the opposite party. It is a very intellectual way of delaying the case as deciding the application before the court consume time and in this way his client is benefited. There are some other group of lawyer, they are successful in his profession also takes false plea for taking dates which is not been considered as a good gesture and also against to the professional ethics, but his client is benefited. But I will suggest not to do all that things which are professionally, ethically and legally not correct. Therefore if the client's interest is satisfied, advocates get more briefs by their recommendation, as I have already told "money begets money but clients beget clients and money both" , if you are working in the best interest of your clients in a professional, ethical and legal way.

Use of technology

Using technology nowadays is very-very important for professionals like an advocate, because the technology always helps you to be faster and smarter in your profession. To understand the benefit of technology, with some example, you may take example of manual typewriting and the computer typewriting; obviously computer typewriting has so many advantages over the manual typewriting. In computer typewriting you may correct or edit your sentences of your pleadings or drafting very easily and you may use this typed part for future use also. Now technology has come to your hand. Your one smart phone is very smart to make you to be in contact with whole world. Google, whatsapp, facebook, twitter and other social networking site is not only for your entertainment but it has also become a means to contact large number of people. Your smart phone is also knowledge box, for your searching activities through internet. You can also store different types of information in the memory card of your mobile. You may store some important acts and judgement of the higher courts in which you are mostly dealing. You may create your small library for your ready reckoner in your mobile this is called the use of technology in the development of your profession. I think advocate should have knowledge of operating computer, scanner, printer, photocopy machine, smart phone etc. We see that most of the offices of government or Non governmental department are providing services through online. It has become necessary for an advocate to have the knowledge of functioning of internet so that he can avail the benefits in his profession. If you are working in field of Tax laws then without knowledge of technology and internet you can not move ahead as every thing is online there and you also have to work online like for registration for GST, filing the return of GST and Income tax, for Pan Card and other services of any organization. Even in High Court and Supreme Court, online filing of the case has been started which require knowledge of technology. Technology helps you to save time. Now you can type any thing through your speech by using voice to type software which is available free of cost by using technology and internet and you can also save your much more time. Technology helps you to develop your relationship and networking. Technology helps you to tell views to whole world at large. You can develop yourself as a successful professional for that you can create your own blog in internet to write on the legal matters. You can start your own YouTube channel on legal topic, so that your capability will be known to the people of the society. After creating blog and YouTube material, you can share it to the social media like Facebook, Twitter, Instragram etc. to develop your marketplace of your profession, as you can not advertise for your profession. In this way we see that technology plays a vital role for developing the profession of advocacy. Infrastructures and a lawyer For a lawyer to have proper infrastructure is very-very important. Most of the time, clients are first impressed by the infrastructure a lawyer have, than it comes to the capability of a lawyer. But it does not mean that if you don't have good infrastructure, you may not become good or a successful advocate. It means if your financial position allows you to have these very things for your professional work, then you must have it, which gives very positive impression in the mind of clients and they start thinking you as a successful professional at a first instance, whether even you don't have a single brief. But here I don't want to demoralize the man coming from a low economic background to this profession, for them also I have different tips to be a successful lawyer. For infrastructure of a lawyer three things are very-very important. First is office, second is library and third is vehicle (motorcycle or car) for movement. So if you are not fortunate enough to have these three things, while you start your profession, you don't dishearten yourself, if you don't afford these things on rent, even then you don't be disheartened yourself. If you are living in your own house then transform your one of the rooms as your office and also start purchase books and make sure that you will invest at least 20% of your earning on books at the initial stage of your profession, then you will see that after few years you have a library may it be small but it will give you office a very professional look. If you don't have your own house then you may do the same thing in rented premises also. Even you are not so fortunate to have this sort of rented house and you are living in a single room on rent basis then my advice is that you decorate that room in such a way that it will look like your office not your home and you can do that very well by applying your mind and do the same as suggested above. When you have first two things, that is office and library, then you start thinking for the third that is your own vehicles, motorcycle or car because your own transport facility will give you a very good opportunity to be in the contact of the people of your society.

A lawyer's ten commandments and the seven lamp of Advocacy

Author concern to lawyer's Ten Commandments and the Seven Lamp of Advocacy very well described this. I am giving here the points only. Here I am not describing about all the points as the words written itself describing and there is no difficulty to understand it by the legal professional who already completed at least his / her bachelors decree in law. A lawyer's Ten Commandments

i.Duties to clients

ii. Neither underestimate or overestimate the value of advice and services.

iii. Duty to court

iv. Do not depend on bluff or trick or pull to win a case

v. Duties to public

vi. Never seek an unjustifiable delay.

vii. Duties to fellow attorneys

viii Do not discuss your case with the court in the absence of opposing counsel.

ix. Duties to self

x. Habit of systematic study

Seven Lamp of Advocacy

i. Honesty

ii. Courage

iii. Industry

iv. Wit

v. Eloquence

vi. Judgment

vii. Fellowship

English language and a legal profession

In the legal profession in India it is very important that you must have command over the English language because the language of proceeding in most of the High Courts and Supreme Court of India is in English. So, command over this language is very much required. If your background of study is other than English medium then you required to focus on your English knowledge. It is not very hard nut to crack, you can learn this very easily by spending some time for this language. When you learn any new language the most important thing is motivation and practice. These two things are not only very essential to learn English language but very important for any work you want to do in your life. So always be motivated and practice this language. Don't be dishearten and feel shy and start thinking any thing in English itself. For improving your spoken English you try to speak this language daily by making your friend, who can accompany you. You must also take care for pronunciations of the words, for that you can develop you habit of listening news in English, watching English movies and serial of your choice. It is always beneficial to watch those movies and serial which story you already know, because it helps you too much to understand it very easily. You should also try to develop your vocabulary, because it is the biggest hurdle to understand this language. Therefore you must keep dictionary while studying so that you can immediately consult, when any word comes, which meaning you are unable to understand. You should not only consult dictionary but also maintained diary to jot down those words for further reference and for memorizing. If you make this habit then within a year you will feel that you have developed yourself very much. Reading English newspaper and magazines will also help you in this regard. I will also suggest learning and practicing tense and sentencing structure formation in English and reading it and practice it on regular basis. You may also join English speaking or group discussion classes. There you get the environment and motivation also. While you speak, you don't bother about your mistakes at the initial phase and go on speaking without any hesitations. By doing all this you see that you become capable enough to write and speak English very well.

Market your Profession

Here market your profession does not mean that you taglines for your cooperation to get a brief for get a brief for hiring any person to market for you for bringing Brave market is not allowed for an advocate in India under the Advocate act games to the professional ethics of a lawyer in fact market your profession there means self in all shot of activities through which you may come in contact with large number of people of your society these activities are become the member of any social organization or club you may become the participants of any religious or cultural activities or you may be one of the organiser of these activities all these are the activities which brings you in contact with a large number of people when they come to know they come into your contact then obviously he will also come to know about your profession you may create your own network of prospective client you can also start your own NGO or trust for doing any social activities indeed hey you may get some monetary help also from 8 member or by the society also by raising and by getting donation from the people in this way it's gift you a wide origin For spreading your contact event without spending money from your own pocket organising program for any social cause than the other organization institution or company may stand beside you to provide you the helping hand there are when you make that the whole sponsorship of the program joining a political party is also a fruitful game for a lawyer which provide injustice it remember don't miss greeting card with you and if you if any person demand you must give them if you will give any person your visiting card then in me location you will find that some other people will also be your memory card which way you come in contact with many person remember please do not give your visiting card to anyone because in that situation your good impression it you want to give your visiting car in but then you have to create a such a situation that you may offer him you your visiting card so that your dignity and Prestige is protected

Know Your Judge

This is also very important in advocacy to know your judges before them you are appearing. That does not mean that you should know your judge personally, but to know about their aptitude and inclination. To make it more clear, inclination of judge is as for example in a rent matter case judge's inclination is towards landlord side or renter side. Whether he is sympathetic towards workman or towards employer, in case of industrial dispute matter. Why you have to understand your judges and their inclination towards which side is due to the reason that after all judges are not a God and is a human being. All those qualities which other human being possess is possessed by the judges also. Not only that you should be very careful to their body language and moods. Personal observation and remark of judges may described here a matter was going on judge opposite side without understanding mood and body language and listening it started arguing the matter for showing his ability then SS chains and fix the date for lifting although they were dismissing the case in favour of opposite party

CHAPTER SIX
Other Considerations

6.Other Considerations
"The safety of the people shall be the highest law"
– Marcus Tullius Cicero

Try to get Retainer ship and Panel

Retainer ship means that client pays a lawyer a small amount on a regular basis, in return of legal services done by the advocate, whenever any need arises by the client. This retainer services by the lawyer is generally taken by any individual who are in need of lot of legal work or by a businessman Who need constant legal work but do not have enough money to hire a lawyer on full time basis. This helps you in your profession as it gives you regular income on regular time basis. While you inter into retainer ship agreement then it is better that you make a written agreement, so that chances of dispute to be arise in future may be minimised. You must be very clear regarding your service to be offered to the client and the fee you will be getting for your service. Like retainer ship in a legal profession there is a word Panel for a lawyer it is nothing but a list of a lawyers made by governmental, non-governmental private company and other institution which get their legal work done by the lawyers who are in the list of their panel. They took the Advocate in their penal for 3 to 5 years as per their requirement and which may be extended. The fee for legal work is decided on the basis of case tackled by a lawyer that is he is given fee per case basis in this case unlike retainer ship where a lawyer get free on regular basis. Mostly banks, insurance company legal service authority and Central Government NGOs and some other private organizations hire advocate on making its panel. For making you clearer I am providing you a notice by the Canara bank for empanelment of advocate which is as follows.

Empanelment of advocates Entrustment of cases:

a) To be eligible for empanelment, the advocate should have minimum five years of actual practice in civil / criminal side, and an office at the place where empanelment is sought.

b) The circle head is vested with the power to empanel advocate in banks Panel for its branches. The branch-in-charge should forward the request for empanelment to R & L / legal section of circle office who, in turn shall place it before the circle Head for order.

c) While recommending for empanelment of an advocate, the branch /R & L / Legal Section of circle office should certify should about the general opinion on efficiency, integrity and respectability of the Advocate ascertained through discreet enquiries at the legal area / Bar / Banks valued customers etc.

d) Efficiency competency and integrity should be the main criteria for appointment as Banks panel advocate. The advocate should be agreeable to banks terms and conditions regarding payment of fee, charges, submission of pleadings / petition for approval etc.

e) Before entrustment of cases to advocate, branch should seek permission of concerned follow-up authority at circle office / head office. R & L section, circle office / DRT liaison office shall ensure that cases are uniformly distributed among panel advocates depending on the nature of cases, complexity involved in each case, performance of Advocates, their availability, vicinity, the capacity to complete cases expeditiously, timely reporting / proper conduct of cases etc

f) Free and other charges shall be as per Bank rule.

g) Panel Advocate should not use Bank's name, symbol etc in their letter head, sign board, name plate, pamphlets etc such as legal advisor to Canara Bank / Advocate for Canara Bank etc.

h) Panel advocate shall not appear / advice against any branch / office of the bank under any circumstances.

i) Inclusion of name in the bank panel shall not constitute an appointment or a right for an appointment to be made by the bank and that Bank reserve its right to terminate that engagement at any time.

j) The Bank is free to comply Advocate of its own

choice and no right exists for an empanelled advocate to claim that he alone should be entrusted with bank work.

k) Bank shall review the performance of panel advocate every year.

l) If panel advocate has committed professional misconduct or has indulged in any act which is against to the professional ethics or has felicitated fraud / perpetration of fraud, R & L Section, circle office shall take steps to lodge complaint with the Bar council concerned for appropriate action.

FEE PAYABLE TO ADVOCATE I.

IN DRT CASES

a) for matter before DRT the fee payable may be fixed at 1% of the claim amount with minimum of Rupees 12,500/- and maximum limit of Rupee 30,000/-. In metro cities, viz Delhi Mumbai Chennai Kolkata and Bangalore the maximum limit shall be Rupee 50,000/-

b) If in any state the scale of fee payable to the Advocate is less than Rupees 30,000/- then scale of fee as per the Civil rule practice in that region alone should be paid and not Rupees 30,000/- or Rupees 50,000/- as stated above.

c) While entrusting the case to advocate, 50% of the fee can be paid. When the claim petition is disposed

off, the balance 50% can be paid. No junior fee is
payable for handling DRT cases.

II. OTHER CASES

The fee payable to advocate shall be on the basis of
the schedule devised by respective circle offices. Thus
by going through the above notice of Canara Bank for
Empanelment of Advocates, it is very clear to you
regarding the empanelment process by the bank, his
requirement and his expectations from the Advocate
entrusted cases of the bank. In this way you can
groom yourself, develop yourself for your perfection
in handling cases of the bank. It is worth mentioning
here that your efficiency, integrity and respectability
count very much to get empanelment as a lawyer not
only in bank but other institutions also.

Client handling /

management

The art of handling or managing clients are very-very important for a profession of an advocate. To be the expert in this matter you have to talk on not only on clients case but try to know about their background, economic condition and educational background their family and relative status etc. But it should not seem him / her that, you are more interested to know about their background instead of knowing his / her case.

You should be very careful while gathering this information. From all those information you will have a better idea for fixing your fee structure to your client. Those who can pay you more and you ask them less fee, the client will not come to you again to get his / her work done, because in that case he / she becomes the suspicious about you and start undermining your capability and if you ask for higher free to your client even then he / she will also not come to you for getting his / her work done, because they are helpless to pay you. You have to handle your client very tactfully. Not only this, you have to understand the feeling and emotions of your client also. You must be aware that their emotions and feelings are not hurt. You have to manage them in such a manner that you may not lose your professional gain. It can be said that you should have knowledge of psychology for dealing your clients in best way. Particularly in family matter your behaviour towards client count much more, as lots of emotions and feelings are attached with this type of cases.

Advocate and Godfather

Like any other profession, this profession of advocacy

also have lots of advantages of having father or a godfather in this profession. The most important thing in any profession is work which comes to you as a professional person. Because you may not be a successful professional even having intelligence and capability with you because you have no place to show them, if you have no case in your hand. In this profession brief or a case does not come to you when you start your career. It takes time. There are so many cases where advocates had to wait 2-3 years to get their first brief. So in those circumstances if you do not have your father or Godfather in this profession your initial time is also wasted and you pass your time without learning or earning. But if you have that opportunity, then you start learning and earning from the beginning itself. Beside this you are also recognize within your professional circle, which gives you professional benefit in the long run. Therefore my suggestion to the young lawyer entering into the profession is that make your 'resume', and try to contact different advocates, whether known to you or not, is not a matter but you try to reach every good and successful lawyer of your area and ask them to join him / her. If he / she gives you opportunity then its fine, if not, you have not to be worried. Try to another lawyers or law chamber. In this way you will be known among your colleague lawyers. They also come to know that you are trying to join any lawyer or law chamber, then if any vacancy arises, in that case they will also help you. Remember you discipline, manner and politeness always work positively in the upliftment of your career in law. This is the main key

to get blessings from you guide or a senior and so
called as your godfather in the long run

Field work Office work and Court work

A lawyers work can be classified into three classes namely field work, office work and court work. The most important among these are field work, which can be called as beginning of the work, because it is that work which is responsible for the brief or case comes to you. If you do more field work, more brief comes to you but you may not be a successful lawyer only by bringing brief through your field work. But you also need to carry out your office work and court work properly. Here the field work means your overall activity like meeting people attending any function, seminar etc which is outside your house, office or court. Office work means your all documentary activities like drafting your case and writing letters to different people, client and organizations etc and also advising government or other authority when any suggestions are invited from them. You may also write to different authorities, organizations or body regarding any social problem related to your locality, your state and your nation. These all sort of work will come under the heading office work, as you do all this in your office and which helps you to increase your contact and face value among the people. Third work is court work for that you must be prepared to argue your case before the Court. Advocate should also be very punctual should be present before the court in time. It is advisable to come to the court campus 30 minutes before. In those circumstances you can not miss your case at any cost. Along with that you develop good reputation before your client, because without an advocate client is helpless and nervous. Beside these works, file management of your case file is also very-very important as you have short span of time to put your case before the court. So your file or related books should be properly flagged, so that your time is not wasted, to search a required documents.

Morning habits of successful person

There are six morning habits of successful man, can be represented by a word SAVERS. First S represent for silence. Most of the people immediately after getting up start taking tension and stress for lot of things. Take tension to read newspaper some other to watch news on television or any serial, some other people are busy in social media Facebook WhatsApp etc, but the successful people do not take any tension like that after getting up in the morning. They are away from all those things written above. They go in a silent mode like doing meditation, yoga, prayer etc. which keep their brain calm make them ready for its better performance. It was found by research that meditation helped many successful people moved ahead in their life to become a successful. So it is very important to practice silence after getting up in the morning. Second A stand for Affirmation. Affirmation is nothing but a positive statement which we say to our self again and again so that it gets struck to our subconscious mind. If you want to write a book then you have to tell yourself every morning that you have to write and publish a book when you do this affirmation daily to yourself it will slowly get struck to your mind, and you start doing so. Third V for Visualization. Visualization is somewhat similar to affirmation. Affirmation again and again to yourself with imagining the affirmed incidence. As you imagine that you have written a book like any other book with having different chapters and a particular design and shape of the book and you also imagine it to be published by a particular publisher. Thus we see that there is a minor difference between affirmation and visualization. In this way in visualization / imagination you think about the things reality and form its image in your brain. Fourth is E for Exercise. There are many benefits of doing early morning exercise it not only make your body feel well and relaxed and empower you not only for better physical work but it also gives your brain a better strength as your brain releases certain hormones which clear your thinking and help you enhance your energy level. For getting all this benefit you do not required to go outside in any ground or gym. It can be achieved just by doing few minutes exercise early in the morning in your house. For this you can even do jumping and do some yoga. Fifth is R which stands for Reading. Reading means to read book which help you to grow and develop, which help you to improve your intelligence, knowledge and improve yourself professionally. Paper or story reading from nobles will not help you. You select reading those books which are very useful for your profession and overall development. Successful person keep himself updated in his work. To become a successful person you make it your habit as a part of your life. Just reading good books even for 15 minutes a day may provide you so many information / knowledge in one year which you can not imagine. Six S stand for Scribing. Scribing means writing your dreams or your goal is something very unique and different. This writing is very powerful which helps you to convert your dreams into reality. Your thoughts are your Idea or knowledge which helps you to much to become a successful man. Therefore it is advisable that kindly keep pen and paper with you so that you may write your thought at the time of its inception.

Night habits of successful person

First wind down before going to bed. You have to

prepare your brain that you are going to sleep and you have to make your subconscious mind ready that you are going to sleep. So it is not advisable work at the last moment you are going to sleep. It is advisable to switch off all your gadgets much early when you are going to sleep. Second before going to sleep you must be relaxed. You may read any sort of book like fictions, biographies etc and reduces your stress and progressively calm your mind. Third is meditation. To do meditation for 5 to 10 minutes before going to sleep is also very beneficial in your life even some exercise can also be done. Fourth Affirmation and visualisation. It is advisable that even before going to bed you should do affirmation and visualize the thing you are going to get in your life as described in morning habits. You have to repeat the same in night habits also. Fifth is to organising yourself for your next day work. For that you must write down your task and that tasks should be meaningful and you should make commitment to do that. You should always try to do all those things for the next day task. Six is set a time to wake up. One should fix his time for waking up. Suppose you want to wake up at 6 a.m., then in that case you have to prepare your mind that you have to wake up at 6 o'clock in the morning. When you develop your habit of waking up early in the morning you will even without taking help of alarm you can wake, as a natural alarm start working for you. Before going to sleep you should also do one thing i.e. to arrange your all items to be used for your next day work and make your beg ready for next day office.

Lawyers and other work

To start earning and maintaining your family from advocacy is not a joke. Because this profession cannot provide you money from day one, like joining any employment. It requires lot of patience. It grows with a span of time that is why lawyer's profession is called a royal profession because it is not for those who want to earn money for running and maintaining his family, as per my opinion. For the first five years this profession is very difficult in terms of earning money. Therefore if you are not coming from a sound economic family, it is very tough in the initial stage. Advocates profession is regulated by Advocates Act and Bar Council of India Rules. Being a lawyer you cannot work in any company or organizations. You cannot even Run your business; you cannot take full time employment. Under Bar Council of India rule you are allowed to do teaching. You are also allowed to do journalism and you are also allowed to be a director of the company but not a Managing Director. Therefore in the initial stage you are unable to earn money as required to maintain your family. You may also have some other option apart from as described above for teaching or journalism, do your business by making a private limited company along with your wife or mother or other members of your family but you should not be the Managing Director, if you really want to be in this profession despite your low earning in initial stage. I would like to suggest you better to opt for teaching law part time in any Law College and to Law student preparing for judicial and other law related examination. Because this teaching will help you in your legal profession also or you may opt for legal journalism for earning money, because these profession and your legal profession can go side by side without any injury. Besides teaching and journalism you can also opt for investing in shares and property which can give you passive earning. You will not have to involve too much for getting earning. But if you are not interested in all those area you may go for in business, but the condition is that you have to make private limited company and you should not be a Managing Director. For doing any business, I would suggest you to do that sort of business in which you are not actively involved. Business which can be done by employing some other person. If you are living in a city where rental income can be generated from property, then you can invest money in constructing house for rent is the best income for you as you are not involved in the business but money / income is generated in regular interval. If you are not inclined for teaching or journalism or business but you are interested in social activities then you can start an NGO by creating society or trust under society Registration Act or Trust Act and take some certification from income tax department like 12 A 80g 35ac and home ministry FERA certification. This certification helps you for taking domestic as well as foreign contribution for your NGO. An advocate shall not personally engage in any business but he may be a sleeping partner in a firm doing business provided that in the opinion of the bar council the nature of the business is not inconsistent with the dignity of the profession and an advocate may be director or chairman of any company with or without any ordinary sitting fee provided none of his duties are of executive character. He shall not be a managing director or a secretary of any company. Advocate shall not be in a full time employment of any person government or corporation. Advocate who has inherited or succeeded by survivorship to a family business may continue it but may not personally participate in the management there of he may continue to hold a share with others in any business which has by the survivorship for inheritance law by will provided. He does not personally participate in the management there of and advocate may Review parliamentary bill for remuneration edit legal tax book at a salary, to do press venting for newspaper, coach people for legal examination, set and examine question papers and subject to the rule against advertising and full time employment, may be in broadcasting journalism, lecturing and teaching legal and non legal subjects. Bar council may allow an advocate from accepting, after obtaining the consent of the state bar council part time employment provided that in the opinion of the state bar council the nature of the employment does not conflict with his professional work and is not inconsistent with the dignity of the profession. Thus looking into these rules of Bar Council of India, you may decide your activity among as described above if you urgently require money to maintain yourself and your family in the initial stage of your legal profession.

Office of an Advocate

An advocate is a person who speaks, writes or acts in defence of another person or organization, usually in a court of law. The name sometimes alternates with terms such as lawyer, counsel or attorney or barrister as spoken in England. An advocate plays an important role in the workplace because he deals with legal issues and may use his knowledge and expertise to assist his clients whether workers or the employer, any other person or organization, in need of legal assistance. His duties and responsibilities varies. Legally speaking an advocate is the person who is authorised by the law to act, appear, defend or plead for another or assist the court. He also gives legal advice, draw pleading or affidavits or other conveyancing deeds. An advocate is the officer of the court like judge, clerk, bailiff, sheriff or the like as he is helpful in upholding the law and administration. He assist the court by presenting views of the client's case before the court but he is not the mouthpiece of his client. He also assists the court in not falling into error of judgement while administrating law and justice to the parties of the case. His statement given before the court is very valuable and court also accept his statement as true as given as statement at the bar. He owes greater responsibilities toward court, client, and colleague and towards society and considered as the learned person of the society. An advocate stands in a loco parentis towards the litigant and his act towards his client otherwise than with utmost good faith is unprofessional. When a person consult a layer for his legal advice, he relies upon his requisite experience, skill and knowledge as lawyer and the lawyer is expected to give proper and passionate legal advice to the client for the protection of his interest. It is professionally improper for an advocate to prepare false documents or to draw pleading knowing that the allegation made is untrue to his knowledge.

Scandalous and obscene question asked by the lawyer to the witness is considered a very weak part of advocate's personality. He also has to keep away from unnecessary strike and his relationship with his clients is of trust and confidence. Along with helping in administration of justice advocates also have duties towards various person which are covered under the Bar council of India Rule also

Printed in Great Britain
by Amazon